GRASSLAND
ECOSYSTEMS

by Tammy Gagne

12 STORY LIBRARY

www.12StoryLibrary.com

12-Story Library is an imprint of Bookstaves and Press Room Editions

Produced for 12-Story Library by Red Line Editorial

Photographs ©: Volodymyr Burdiak/Shutterstock Images, cover, 1; kungfoofoto/Shutterstock Images, 4; GreenBelka/Shutterstock Images, 5; Tom Reichner/Shutterstock Images, 6, 7; Foto 4440/Shutterstock Images, 8, 9; TasiPas/Shutterstock Images, 10; Hurghea Constantin/Shutterstock Images, 11; Wolf Avni/Shutterstock Images, 12; Benjamin B/Shutterstock Images, 13; Tero Hakala/Shutterstock Images, 14; John Carnemolla/Shutterstock Images, 15; Fernando Castelani/Shutterstock Images, 16, 29 (top right); Sergey Uryadnikov/Shutterstock Images, 17, 28 (top); TTphoto/Shutterstock Images, 18; Kletr/Shutterstock Images, 19; Ian Rentoul/Shutterstock Images, 20; NickEvansKZN/Shutterstock Images, 21; Sanit Fuangnakhon/Shutterstock Images, 22; rmfox/iStockphoto, 23; Patrick Jennings/Shutterstock Images, 24; Marso/Shutterstock Images, 25; ESB Professional/Shutterstock Images, 26; Lucky Business/Shutterstock Images, 27; rkraan/iStockphoto, 28 (middle); WLDavies/iStockphoto, 28 (bottom), 29 (bottom left); czekma13/iStockphoto, 29 (top left); 1001slide/iStockphoto, 29 (bottom right)

Content Consultant: Benjamin F. Tracy, Associate Professor, Department of Crop and Soil Environmental Sciences, Virginia Tech

Library of Congress Cataloging-in-Publication Data
Names: Gagne, Tammy, author.
Title: Grassland ecosystems / by Tammy Gagne.
Description: Mankato, MN : 12-Story Library, 2018. | Series: Earth's
  ecosystems | Includes bibliographical references and index. | Audience:
  Grade 4 to 6.
Identifiers: LCCN 2016047632 (print) | LCCN 2016053519 (ebook) | ISBN
  9781632354570 (hardcover : alk. paper) | ISBN 9781632355232 (pbk. : alk.
  paper) | ISBN 9781621435754 (hosted e-book)
Subjects: LCSH: Grassland ecology--Juvenile literature.
Classification: LCC QH541.5.P7 G34 2018 (print) | LCC QH541.5.P7 (ebook) |
  DDC 577.4--dc23
LC record available at https://lccn.loc.gov/2016047632

Printed in China
022017

Access free, up-to-date content on this topic plus a full digital version of this book. Scan the QR code on page 31 or use your school's login at 12StoryLibrary.com.

Table of Contents

Weather Greatly Affects Grassland Ecosystems 4

The Prairies Provide Food for North America 6

The Pampas Spread Across Argentina 8

The Steppe Spans Two Continents 10

The Veld Has Become South Africa's Farmland 12

Australia's Rangelands Are Part of the Outback 14

Savanna Ecosystems Are Tropical Grasslands 16

Grassland Plants Provide Food for Many Animals 18

Grassland Animals Graze or Hunt to Survive 20

Wildfires Can Be Good for Grassland Ecosystems 22

People Have Taken Over Many Grassland Areas 24

People Can Save the Grasslands 26

Grasslands Food Web 28

Glossary 30

For More Information 31

Index 32

About the Author 32

Weather Greatly Affects Grassland Ecosystems

A group of living things and their environment is called an ecosystem. Grassland ecosystems are found on every continent except Antarctica. There are many types of grasslands. Each one is important in its own way.

Weather plays a big role in the grasslands. The amount of rain sets grassland ecosystems apart from others. Grasslands do not get as much rain as forests. This is why few trees grow in grasslands. But grasslands are not as dry as deserts.

There are different types of grasslands. Tropical grasslands are found closest to the equator. These regions are warm all year. They receive heavy rain during the summer. They become drier during the other seasons. The African

Many grassland ecosystems are used as farmland.

−40

Degrees, in Fahrenheit (−40°C), of the lowest temperature in the temperate grasslands during an average winter.

- The amount of rain a grassland ecosystem receives affects it greatly.
- Grasslands get more rain than deserts but not as much as forests.
- Tropical grasslands are warm year-round and have both a wet and a dry season.
- Temperate grasslands have a dormant time when nothing grows.

Grasslands cover approximately a quarter of the planet.

THINK ABOUT IT

Based on the information you have read here, do you think grasslands are more like forests or deserts? Give evidence to support your answer.

savanna is a tropical grassland ecosystem.

Temperate grasslands get less rain than tropical grasslands. Precipitation can vary between 10 and 30 inches (25 and 76 cm) a year. Some of it falls as snow during winter. The grass in temperate regions tends to be shorter than in tropical grasslands. In some areas, grasses may be less than one inch (2.5 cm) tall. North America's Great Plains are temperate grasslands.

Farmers grow crops in both tropical and temperate grasslands. But the temperate region has a shorter growing season. A dormant season follows. During this time, it is too cold or dry for any plants to grow.

2

The Prairies Provide Food for North America

The Great Plains of the United States and Canada have the largest amount of prairie land in North America. Prairies are flat grasslands found across the United States, including Colorado, Kansas, Montana, Nebraska, New Mexico, North Dakota, Oklahoma, South Dakota, Texas, and Wyoming. The Great Plains also extend into the Canadian provinces of Alberta, Manitoba, and Saskatchewan.

The prairies serve as farmland for the continent. The grasses that cover much of the land hold soil in place. The weather can be harsh. But the prairie grasses keep soil from eroding. Crops people use for

Prairie dogs are a common sight on North American prairies.

Bison graze on grasslands in the United States and Canada.

food, such as wheat, rye, and oats, thrive in the Great Plains.

Prairies help improve water quality in surrounding areas. In most places, rainwater washes sediment into rivers and streams. Prairies trap sediment before it can travel to these waterways. In this way, grasslands act as a natural water filter.

Prairies provide habitats for many plants and animals. The tall grasses are food for large animals, such as antelope and deer. They also shelter small animals, such as birds and gophers, from predators.

1,400,000
Land, in square miles (3,625,983 sq km), covered by prairies in North America.

- The Great Plains are located in the United States and Canada.
- Farmers use this prairie land to produce large amounts of food, such as wheat, rye, and oats.
- Prairie grasses help keep waterways clean by trapping sediment.
- Grasses serve as food and shelter for many animals.

The Pampas Spread Across Argentina

The pampas of South America are some of the largest grassland areas in the world. These plains are found mainly in Argentina. They cover 295,000 square miles (764,000 sq km) of land. The pampas stretch from the Atlantic coast to the foothills of the Andes Mountains.

The weather in some grasslands changes with the seasons. But the weather in the pampas depends on the location. The western side of this ecosystem is dry like a desert. In the east, the air is more humid. Warm winds from the north often mix with cool air from the south to produce more rain in this region.

Sunflowers grow in the pampas in South America.

12

Height, in feet (3.7 m), pampas grass can grow.

- The pampas grasslands cover a large area in Argentina.
- The weather in the pampas is dry in the west and humid in the east.
- The rich soil in the pampas is made up of clay, silt, and sand.
- The pampas produce much of the food in South America.

The pampas produce a large amount of food for the South American people. Farmers grow alfalfa, wheat, corn, and soybeans. The pampas are also known for their vineyards. The western city of Mendoza, Argentina, produces half of all the wines that come from South America.

The soil in the pampas is richer than soil found in most other places. It is made mostly of clay. It also contains fine sand and silt. These materials are carried into the grasslands by waterways and dust storms. The soil is ideal for farming because it holds moisture very well.

The pampas gray fox roams the South American grasslands.

Many wild animals live in the pampas. Foxes, pumas, and a member of the camel family called the guanaco are just a few species that share this ecosystem. The number of cattle in the region is also high. Cattle eat much of the grass in the pampas. They leave little for the many wild herbivores that live in this region.

The Steppe Spans Two Continents

The Eurasian Steppe is a large grassland that spans two continents. It reaches from Hungary in Europe to China in Asia.

A mountain range breaks the steppe into two sections. The Western Steppe begins near the Danube River in Hungary and extends eastward to Asia's Altai Mountains. Rainfall and temperatures are milder in the westernmost parts. The steppe in Ukraine and nearby Romania has some of the world's best farmland. This is due to the good climate and rich soils.

Steppe ecosystems can be found near the Altai Mountains in Siberia.

Pheasant's eye grows in the Eurasian steppe.

The Eastern Steppe begins on the other side of the Altai Mountains in Mongolia. It extends east to the Greater Khingan Mountains in northeast China. This part of the ecosystem is much colder and drier than the Western Steppe. For these reasons, grass in this region is shorter and sparser.

5,000

Distance, in miles (8,047 km), from the western edge of the Western Steppe to the eastern edge of the Eastern Steppe.

- The Eurasian Steppe reaches from Hungary to China.
- Asia's Altai Mountains divide the Eurasian Steppe into two sections.
- The weather conditions are milder in the westernmost parts of the steppe.
- The Eastern Steppe is just warm and wet enough to grow small amounts of grass.

CONNECTING THE EAST TO THE WEST

The Eurasian Steppe has a long and rich history. For many years, it was one of the most important travel and trade routes between Europe, India, and China. Before modern transportation, people rode horses, donkeys, and camels through this region. A route running through the Steppe called the Silk Road has been used since 200 BCE.

11

The Veld Has Become South Africa's Farmland

South Africa is home to a grassland ecosystem called the veld. This land is used mostly for farmland. The grasses that grow in this region are sweeter than the grasses that grow in nearby countries. They are often called sweetveld for this reason. Livestock prefer sweetveld to sour-tasting grasses. Farmers grow most of South Africa's corn in the veld. The area is known for corn and livestock.

The veld receives more rain during summer than it does in winter. The air temperature can vary from

THINK ABOUT IT

Think about the information you have read here. What might happen to certain grass species in the veld if farmers use more land to plant crops? Find a sentence or two to support your answer.

Animals drink at a watering hole in the Zululand veld.

The veld covers vast areas of South Africa.

12 degrees Fahrenheit (−11°C) in winter to 100 degrees Fahrenheit (38°C) in summer.

Because so many people use the veld for farmland, the area is one of the most endangered grasslands in the world. Several grass species that grow naturally in this region do not grow anywhere else in the world. Unique animal species live here, too. A bird called the blue crane is found only in South Africa. Female blue cranes will lay their eggs only in this region. Like the grassland itself, this species is at risk of becoming endangered.

16 to 35
Average yearly rainfall, in inches (41 to 89 cm), in the veld.

- Most of South Africa's veld is used for farmland.
- Grasses that grow in the veld taste sweeter than grasses that grow in nearby countries.
- Temperatures vary greatly in the veld from summer to winter.
- The veld is one of the most endangered grasslands in the world.

Australia's Rangelands Are Part of the Outback

Approximately three-quarters of Australia is made up of grasslands called rangelands. They are found in the northern part of the continent between the states of Western Australia and Queensland. The rangelands are part of a larger area called the Outback.

The rangelands get between 9.8 and 13.8 inches (25 and 35 cm) of rain each year. January, which falls in the middle of Australia's summer, is the wettest month. During summer, temperatures can reach 102 degrees Fahrenheit (39°C). A long dry season follows the summer months. The temperature can dip as low as 48 degrees Fahrenheit (8.9°C).

26 million

Approximate number of beef cattle owned by grasslands ranchers in Australia.

- The rangelands get the most rain during the month of January.
- The dry season in the rangelands is long with cooler temperatures.
- Both wild animals and livestock depend on the rangeland grasses for food.

Much of Australia is covered in grasslands.

Kangaroos are common in the Australian Outback.

A LONG HISTORY

The rangelands are home to Australia's indigenous people, the Aboriginals. Evidence shows that the Aboriginals have lived in these grasslands for as long as 50,000 years. The Aboriginals discovered that burning grasslands helped these ecosystems thrive. It helped control woody plants and weeds and increase plant growth. Burning is still practiced in some parts of Australia.

The grassy rangelands are home to many animals. More than half of Australia's bird species and a third of its mammals are part of this ecosystem. Most of the people who live in the grasslands make their living from ranches. Cattle graze on the grasses, as do wild animals, such as kangaroos and rabbits.

Savanna Ecosystems Are Tropical Grasslands

A grassy plain dotted with trees is called a savanna. This ecosystem is known for being wet in summer and dry in winter. Savannas lie between rainforests and deserts. The air in a savanna is warm all the time.

Giraffes call the African savanna home.

The African savanna is located in several countries. It stretches from Guinea to Ethiopia in central Africa all the way to South Africa. This ecosystem is home to a wide variety of wildlife. Nearly 500 types of birds and 45 mammal species live in this region. It is home to the largest number of hoofed

More than 1 million wildebeests migrate across the savanna each year.

species in the world. The antelope, wildebeest, and rhinoceros are just a few of the hoofed animals that roam the African savanna.

India's savanna ecosystem is known for its tall grasses. Elephant grass often grows as high as 23 feet (7 m) in this region. This plentiful grass provides food for a spotted deer species known as the chital. Bengal tigers also live in this area. They feed on the chital population.

ON THE MOVE

Animals move with the seasons in the African savanna. As the long winter begins, rain comes much less often. Many water sources dry up during this time. Millions of animals migrate north in search of food. Predators follow them. When the summer months and rains return, the animals move southward again.

15 to 25

Average rainfall, in inches (38 to 64 cm), the African savanna gets during summer.

- The savanna links rainforests to deserts.
- The African savanna provides homes for a large range of animal species.
- Elephant grass is an important part of India's savanna ecosystem.

Grassland Plants Provide Food for Many Animals

Grassland ecosystems provide the perfect habitat for grazing animals, such as bison and zebras. The part of grasses that produce new growth is close to the ground. Animals eat only the tops of the grasses. For this reason, the grasses can keep growing even after animals have fed on them.

The structure of grass helps it thrive in the grassland ecosystem. Blades of grass are curved so they can make the most of any rain that falls.

Zebras eat the grasses of the African savanna.

Grasses need rain in order to thrive.

Raindrops slide inward toward the roots, where they are soaked up. Grasses have deep roots. They extend far into the ground below the grass. The roots use the water within the soil to grow.

Grasses are not the only plants found in grassland ecosystems. Flowering plants and shrubs are also common in these regions. Similar to grasses, these plants have deep roots that help them survive in hot or dry climates. The plants in the grasslands adapt easily to the ever-changing environment.

8

Length, in feet (2.4 m), to which the roots of some grass species can grow.

- Grass provides food for many grazing animals.
- The structure of grass helps it keep growing even when rain is limited.
- Grassland plants have deep roots that help them soak up the moisture in soil.
- Flowering plants and shrubs are found in grassland ecosystems.

Grassland Animals Graze or Hunt to Survive

A wide range of animals live in grassland ecosystems. In Africa, zebras and lions occupy the grasslands. In Australia, kangaroos call the grasslands home. Wildlife in North America's grasslands includes badgers, prairie dogs, and wolves. Snakes and termites are also part of grassland ecosystems throughout the world.

Many grassland animals survive by eating plants. Predators on the grasslands include lions or foxes. They survive by hunting herbivores, such as antelope or rabbits. Often the predators are larger than their prey. But this is not always the case. A lion will hunt down a giraffe, especially if the giraffe is young or weak.

Snakes are another type of grassland animal that can be more

Badgers make their homes on dry, open grasslands.

THINK ABOUT IT

One might say that plants are important to all animals in a grassland ecosystem. Based on what you have read, would you agree with this statement? Find sentences that support your answer.

RECORD BREAKERS

The African savanna is home to both the heaviest land animal and the tallest land animal on the planet. The African elephant can weigh up to 14,000 pounds (6,350 kg). The giraffe can stand up to 19 feet (5.8 m) tall. Both species are herbivores.

300

Weight, in pounds (136 kg), of food an African elephant can eat in a single day.

- Many kinds of animals live in grassland ecosystems.
- Herbivores survive by eating grasses and other plants.
- Predators, such as lions and wolves, survive by eating other grassland animals.
- Some of the fiercest animals in the grasslands are not the largest ones.

powerful than they look based on their size. The highly venomous black mamba lives in Africa. It mainly eats birds and small mammals. But it will eat other snakes, too. This species has even been known to eat cobras, one of the deadliest snake species on the planet.

Black mambas live in the grasslands of southern and eastern Africa.

Wildfires Can Be Good for Grassland Ecosystems

Wildfires present a danger to many ecosystems. But fire can be a good thing for grasslands in some cases. Some grasslands would not be able to exist without occasional fires. Fires help prevent trees and other woody plants from taking over in these regions.

When a fire starts, larger animals run away from the blaze. Many small animals, such as insects and reptiles, burrow into the ground to

Sometimes grasslands need fires to help them thrive.

1

Time, in weeks, it takes for the first signs of new grasses to appear after a fire.

- Grasslands depend on fires to keep trees and other woody plants from taking over.
- Fires in grasslands may occur naturally or be set by people.
- Dry, windy conditions help spread fire across grasslands.

Lightning sometimes causes fires on grasslands.

escape the fire. Grass cannot move away from the fire. But it will grow back quickly as long as its roots survive.

Fires often occur naturally in grasslands, especially when the air has been dry for a long time. Lightning is one of the most common fire starters. When it strikes, sparks can cause the grass to catch fire. Landowners also sometimes set fires on purpose. But they are careful to keep them from spreading too far. In both cases, wind often helps spread the flames.

GRASSLAND ECOSYSTEMS THRIVE AFTER FIRES

Many grassland plants grow even better after a fire. The ground protects roots from burning. Ashes from burnt plant matter make excellent fertilizer. With trees and woody plants gone, grasses receive more sunlight following a fire. Some animals also thrive after a fire. Bison, for example, prefer to eat grass from areas that have recently burned.

People Have Taken Over Many Grassland Areas

People have made it harder for many grassland species to survive. Farming, construction, and hunting threaten the grasslands and all the living things within them.

The grasslands have rich soil that makes them ideal for farming. But farms have taken over large parts of these ecosystems. Many grassland areas that are not used for growing crops are used for livestock grazing. Too many grazing animals can hurt grasslands. If they eat too many of the plants, they can turn grasslands into deserts. This is especially true during times of drought. Some grasslands have been bulldozed to build cities. In temperate regions, about 47 percent of the grasslands have been replaced by farms or buildings.

Grasslands are often used for farming.

Overhunting and poaching threaten many animal species in the grasslands. The number of African elephants in the African savanna has greatly declined in recent years. These large animals are very important to the grassland ecosystem. They help keep grasslands free of trees and shrubs by eating them before they can grow too big.

People dig up grasslands for housing and to build cities.

20

Approximate percentage of the European Union that is covered by grasslands.

- Human development has made it difficult for grasslands to thrive.
- Cropland has greatly reduced the amount of grasslands.
- Cities have taken over many grassland areas.
- Overhunting and poaching have reduced many grassland animal populations.

SMALLER GRASSLANDS STRUGGLE TO SURVIVE

Smaller grassland ecosystems have a harder time thriving than larger ones. Problems often start when people move into these smaller ecosystems. People destroy smaller areas faster. Before smaller areas can recover, the construction of more buildings often begins.

People Can Save the Grasslands

Today, the Great Plains take up just 5 percent of the land they once did. Farming and construction are largely to blame. Much of the damage that has been done cannot be undone. But people can save what is left of these important ecosystems.

People can help grasslands by donating money or time to conservation organizations, such as The Nature Conservancy or the World Wildlife Fund. These organizations study and protect the grasslands and other ecosystems. People can write to their government

Grasslands need to be protected to ensure they are around for years to come.

representatives and urge them to help protect these ecosystems. Conservation laws keep people from destroying protected areas. For example, people cannot build on protected grasslands.

Learning more about the grasslands is one of the most important steps in protecting them. Sharing knowledge with others is also important. The more people who know how to help grassland ecosystems, the better the chances of saving them will be.

8

Approximate percentage of grasslands that are protected worldwide.

- Donating to a conservation group that helps protect grasslands is a great way to make a difference.
- Writing to government representatives can help lead to new protection laws.
- Sharing information about conservation with others can help save grassland ecosystems.

Grasslands Food Web

wildebeest

hyena

impala

grass

giraffe

lion

acacia tree

29

Glossary

adapt
Change to fit a situation.

conservation
The act of protecting a natural resource.

dormant
To slow down or become inactive for a period of time.

herbivores
Animals that eat only plants.

poaching
Illegal hunting.

precipitation
Water that falls to the ground as snow or rain.

predators
Animals that hunt other animals for food.

sediment
Stones and sand deposited by water.

silt
Small material carried by a river that settles on the bottom or near the mouth of a waterway.

venomous
Producing poison that can be delivered through a bite or sting.

vineyards
Fields of grapevines used to make wine.

For More Information

Books

Bow, James. *Grasslands Inside Out*. New York: Crabtree Publishing, 2015.

Higgins, Melissa. *Grassland Ecosystems*. Minneapolis: Abdo Publishing, 2016.

Silverman, Buffy. *Grassland Food Chains*. Chicago: Heinemann, 2011.

Visit 12StoryLibrary.com

Scan the code or use your school's login at **12StoryLibrary.com** for recent updates about this topic and a full digital version of this book. Enjoy free access to:

- Digital ebook
- Breaking news updates
- Live content feeds
- Videos, interactive maps, and graphics
- Additional web resources

Note to educators: Visit 12StoryLibrary.com/register to sign up for free premium website access. Enjoy live content plus a full digital version of every 12-Story Library book you own for every student at your school.

Index

Africa, 4, 12–13, 16–17, 20, 21, 25
Altai Mountains, 10–11
Andes Mountains, 8
Argentina, 8–9
Asia, 10
Australia, 14–15, 20

Bengal tigers, 17
bison, 18, 23
blue cranes, 13

cattle, 9, 15
China, 10–11
construction, 24, 25, 26
crops, 5, 6, 24

deer, 7, 17

Eurasian Steppe, 10, 11
Europe, 10, 11

farming, 5, 6, 9, 10, 12–13, 24, 26
fires, 15, 22–23
foxes, 9, 20

giraffes, 20, 21
Great Plains, 5, 6–7, 26

livestock, 12, 24

North America, 5, 6, 10, 20

Outback, 14

pampas, 8–9
prairie dogs, 20
prairies, 6–7

rangelands, 14–15
roots, 19, 23

savanna, 5, 16–17, 21, 25
snakes, 20–21
soil, 6, 9, 10, 19, 24
South America, 8–9
steppe, 10–11

temperate grasslands, 5, 24
tropical grasslands, 4–5, 16–17

United States, 6

veld, 12–13

zebras, 18, 20

About the Author

Tammy Gagne has written more than 150 books for both adults and children. She resides in northern New England with her husband and son. One of her favorite pastimes is visiting schools to talk to children about the writing process.

READ MORE FROM 12-STORY LIBRARY

Every 12-Story Library book is available in many formats. For more information, visit 12StoryLibrary.com.